Ruins were Castles

Gursher Singh Randhawa

To order additional copies of this book, contact:
Xlibris
1-888-795-4274
www.Xlibris.com
Orders@Xlibris.com

ISBN: Softcover   978-1-7960-8010-0
         Hardcover   978-1-7960-8011-7
         EBook   978-1-7960-8009-4

Print information available on the last page

Rev. date: 12/27/2019

I am grateful to almighty, my family, Gabbi Foster, Iris Johannsen and Lani Martin for helping me producing this book.

1

Cannot make a
statement at the time.
It's a long time for me.

The lost days are sitting
in the darkness.
I look at my caste now.

Blue pens and blank pages,
These are all I earned.

2

If there were injuries
in your life,
So they said you
were helpless.

The heart was in the heart,
So they said you
were cunning.

If you disclosed the
tale of the heart,
So they said you
were nebbishy.

Now, I am no longer
waiting for anyone.
I am tired, my dear.

3

We together are like
paintings in the museum.
With every passing
moment, the worth
is increasing.

Just like the relation
of land and crop,
Which has gone
or changed with
the past season,
This is an increasing
trend to know.

By touching the autumn
tree, you will go far in
the blooming gardens.

And I will find your
fragrance in my dry,
lifeless leaves.
You may be happy with
our past, so I will run after
your traces in my dreams.
I do not question any
of your words.
I am afraid of your silence.
That same complaint
I do have with me
Because some of my
sentences drench her
with waves of anxiety.
But I am convinced
that this agony will
bring laughter to her
face in the future,
Because time heals
every wound.
For her, respect in my
heart is in same way and
entire life will be there.
I think she is
different from all.
Silence between our lips
was not intimidating,
nor was it scary,
Because I consider
your scarf as mine.

4

The foundation of
the body has never
been mastered
Even after being
habituated to one another.

It will be mastered when
you will find something
lost centuries ago.

It will be mastered when
you will find a shelter
during a tough journey.
It will be mastered when
you will get a shoulder to
cry on among strangers.
It will be mastered when
you forget your valuables
deliberately somewhere.
You will master it when
soft branches of the heart
will be in full blossom.
You will master it
when a stream of
emotions gushes out.
That day, you will be
a master when you
convey the story just
with your eyes.

5

By the delicacy
of my words,
I was recognized by her.
Soaked in the fresh
mist of morning,
Became a guest
in my heart.

Sometimes, there seemed
to be confusing secrets,
Which has become easy
to understand now.

Whenever a smile was
there in response,
I was ruined with
the benefits.
Hearing the mystery of
these verses, clouds of
surprise engulfed her.

6

How could she scarify
my memories?
How could she forgive me?
She agreed with me
in life so far.
How could she stand
against me?
She was deprived
of feathers.

How could she fly high?

Every moment, she
experienced death.
How could a dead
person die?

7

Sitting alone for thousands
of times, I fill my brain up
to my neck with thoughts.
So I would love to be
lonely while standing
in the crowd.
When only I was near me,
I feel I am worthless.

And sometimes, I get
up from the gathering
because I want to
know my valuation.

8

They drew a line, and
skies cried out.
Brothers got separated.
Flowers and thorns
shed tears.
When land got freedom,
Mothers wept over infants.
Our homes became
our graves.

Lovers forgot how to love.

That laughter was
still in there.
They call me in dreams.
I hear everyone is
waiting for me.
Really?

9

I wonder why we
don't recognize the
flower in spring.
I wonder why we don't
inhale the breeze filled
with the freshness
of a new season.

I wonder why we cry
for the voids that were
occupied by those
great ones long ago.

10

Who is going to
define morality?
The one who has made
his parents proud of
him is not moral.
The one who is preaching
day and night is not moral.

Humans will never
behave like the sun. They
will never match the
chemistry and discipline
of the earth and moon.
Nature is the most
moral person ever found
but never speaks.

11

Moving out of illuminated
rooms and sitting in a
box that has wheels and
torches is development?
Collecting material,
gadgets, leaving before
your time and eating
share of brothers sitting
on the other end of planet.
Is this development?

More products and
less time. Is this
what we earned?
Will it be always that
ice-cold regions will get
snow and children of
deserts will never get to
play with snowballs?

Will there be a single
person in a poor nation
who is happier than
most of the persons in a
"developed country"? Will
we be able to find reason
behind his happiness?

12

Sometimes, I get amazed
by things like teens who
will fall in love even in
the twenty-second century
and classic artists who will
be fresh in the twenty-
fifth. Some people and
phenomena are eternal
in an interesting way.

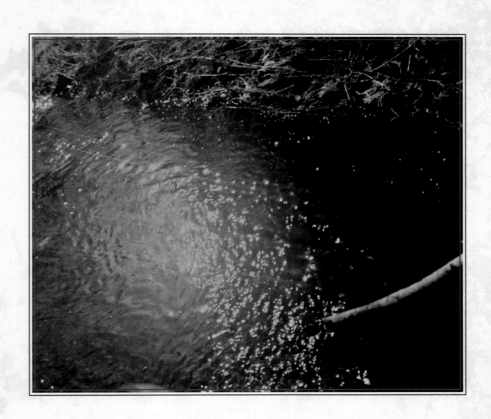

13

We feel low in some
parts of the day and in
different stages of life,
but thinking of the great
persons who made the
impossible possible, who
made it through a handful
of resources, and who
fought against hunger and
thirst will encourage us.

When we wake up at
midnight and grab a bottle
of water while drinking,
when we realize that
those were also humans,
this gives real inspiration
coated with consolation.

14

While walking down the
street, a boy was thinking,
*Have we discovered
everything? Is there nothing
beyond physics, chemistry?*
Or

Do we have to travel back
to our masters of art who
were calm and composed?

15

A boy from the village
came to the city and was
disturbed by his peers.
He talked to himself,
Why are these people not
civilized? Why do they not
speak less or when required?

And then suddenly, a
thought occurred.
Okay, this is what Grandpa
used to call degradation.

16

People generally get
influenced by time, but
then some people are there.
They impact the time.
That phase is remembered
by their name. We have
seen this in families,
cultures, nations, and
continents. But there is a
minute line where they get
a chance to be remembered
as cruel or kind.

17

We were wandering near the coast. Suddenly, a discussion started on gender dominance. She laughed and said, "Men are sure because of mensuration," and I was spellbound over her wit.

18

He was roaming around
on the terrace and having
a conversation with
angels on his shoulder.
"Whenever I go out
with them on a party
or outing, I don't
enjoy it. After coming
back, I feel that I have
wasted something." He
confidently replied to the

angel, "I will start enjoying
my loneliness. I will go to
the places I am interested
in. Nobody knows what
I am searching for."

19

They were talking
about the places they
visit in summers.
And
I was imagining the
city, castle, and cottage
of spirituality where I
am heading toward.

20

We love to classify things.
We love to bracket the
things together. We have
even classified the things
that cannot be without
knowing it, i.e., *time*.

It is different when we
see time on a clock.
It is different when
we see a calendar.
It is different when
we feel nostalgia.
It is different when we
remember our ancestors.
But time is time,
And
We are doing the same
with God. To some
extent, we did that.

21

There was a first moment.
They both were hesitant to
start a conversation. As the
sun kept throwing light
on the planet, similarity of
choices and same reactions
on incidents deepened
that relation. It all ended
when one was attending
the other's funeral.

Friendship is
unpredictable.

22

He tweaked his white
beard and said with
a deep voice,
"At any age, life is always
a weird proportion of
luxury and discomforts."

23

Enlightened person is
controversial in big spheres
of inferiors and small
spheres of superiors.

24

Difference between the
real world and the virtual
world is the same as the
persons and places we
meet and visit as compared
to that we have imagined.

25

I was sailing on the
sea full of tears.
Your memory
was the boat.
I wanted to drown
with you.
I wasted life looking
at people,
And

It hurts because I got it
from the same ones.

26

Those who went
Didn't come back.
Shoulders are heavy.
Why did the heart
get cracked?
Don't lose the spirit.
You belong to the supreme.
Fake laughter on your face,
And pain is extreme.

27

My wounds got worse.
This world is cruel.
I got compelled to
meet enemies.
This world is cruel.
They made me fed
up of relations.
This world is cruel.

My blood is no longer
blood. It is water now.
This world is cruel.

28

We never get absolute
environment or places, but
our ability to cope and
compromise makes it easy.
From another angle, we
do not get ideal persons
because paragon is
rarely materialized.

29

Buckle yourself up. You
do not know where
strength will be used. You
do not know where your
shoulders will be used.
Time is making you the
person your soul can
hold, not the person
you want to become.

So wait for phases
and faces.

30

Technology is like
Father's wealth.

31

Taming

People are like caves. To
look and know what goes
in their minds, you must
enter with a stake of facts.
You will get the rays of
optimism and darkness
where you can see neither
the cave nor yourself.

32

Poles

Two guys sat, and one said,
"Do you feel sometimes
in the morning when
you wake up from sleep
and forget everything
about yourself—what is
the shape of your face?
How tall are you? And
then you come out of the
room and start playing the
role that you have been
playing from a while."
The other said, "Hurry
up. Let's go to the
theater. Otherwise, we
will miss the show."

33

Vulnerable

After ages, I saw her, and
I was looking at her the
way a widow looks at
herself in the mirror.

34

Fenced

Countless lies, truths,
and misunderstandings
need just an enclosure.

35

Embroidered Minds

Some events leave deep
prints on our minds. We
all have a small number
of imprints in our mind
that walk along with us
in our whole lives. We
all can compare and
relate that to our fellows
but cannot describe it,
Like the way I am not
able to describe it here.

36

If we closely analyze our
best friend, there will
be one tragic happening
or amusing episode
that has happened in
one's life around which
that affinity revolves.

37

Focal

Grandpa and his grandson
were sitting under a big
tree in a farmhouse.
Grandpa lay down on
the cot, and the little one
jumped and sat on his
tummy. Grandfather said,
"Your mind should have
the ability to behave like
both convex and concave
lens, i.e., focusing just
on your target and just
spreading and giving
out the relaxation."

38

Humming Angel

Messages to trunks
and your wings
Wherever you come to
greet with your feet.
On the way home,
ask such routes.
Breathe in slowly while
slowly moving.
If not sure, ask the winds
How much they are
slaves of your memories.

Or if I laugh with the
trees of your land,
Let your pearls be
in my garland.
How do I tell you the
fineness of that evening?
You wake up to the
lost thoughts,
Ecstatic to be far away.
Even the poisoned honey
was no harm to the lips.
The thing that has
been gossip is now
a normal thing.
Messages to trunks
and your wings
Wherever you come to
greet with your feet.

39

Deck of Life

You don't know what you
will get. The weakest of
one class becomes heavy
on the heaviest of another.
One saves his assets for
the last section, but just
one wrong move and
everything loses its worth.
Life is just like
hearts, clubs, spades,
and diamonds.

40

Solitude

They were all hardworking
and giving firm statements
to prove it, but he was
circumvolving the
neutral rod of thought.
He was confident in
sitting idle because he
knew what was going
on in the outer world.

Index

W

Y

Printed in the United States
By Bookmasters